BEYOND THE SURFACE

Dorian Petersen Potter

BEYOND THE SURFACE

I want to dedicate this poetry book to God, and to Jesus Christ,
my Lord and my Savior. They had always been in my life
the biggest and greatest inspiration of all.
Thank You God and Jesus for all that You both had
done, and for your most wonderful gift of
love, forgiveness and salvation.

MY HEART

(Jesus Tears)

My
Heart each
Day leaps with
Joy in the Lord
He wants me to walk
Eternally with
Him straight all
The way
Through

I
Do make
Mistakes but
He forgives me
See God when sun glow
In heart praise him
Accept Him
Get his
Peace

I
Wake up
Each morning
And see all the
Beauty He has made
All around us
He gives life
Blessings
Too

~Shining~

(Kyrielle Sonnet)

Stay focus till you reach your goal
Take it slow and watch for your soul
Don't rush and you will be just fine
Know with God's love and help you'll shine

Stay focus in your heart and mind
Do your part remember God's kind
As He has your heart in a shrine
Know with God's love and help you'll shine

God for sure has a plan for you
And always shows all His love true
If you let Him you'll walk the line
Know with God's love and help you'll shine

Stay focus till you reach your goal
Know with God's love and help you'll shine.

~He's In All That's Great and Good~

(Eleventh Power)

When I wake up enjoy what I can today
In worship spend time with God thank Him for all
He gives plenty of blessings to me and you
Praise Him all the time and seek him when I fall
Feel his love today and try walk in his way
He'll protect you always you dont have to crawl
When we put God first in all we will just grow
Under his loving care then our souls will glow
Just have faith and stand in Jesus tall and strong
Devil try block way and bring you only wrong
But with God you defeat devil and sing songs.

~Summer Rainy Days~

(Trinet)

The days
Are hot
Summer months are very humid here
Sometimes rain falls for many days
Heat rises
It then
Gets worse

The sky
Gets darker
Heat can be very oppressive sometimes
People open windows, try keep cool
Rain continues
To fall
For hours

Not cool
Still hot
Rain had fallen constantly all day
The day looks grim and blue
People hurry
Home or
Stay indoors.

~Focus~

(The Minuet)

Stay focus till you reach your dreams
Dreams are so great
Great just to have
Have and enjoy

As you do this you'll start to climb
Climb, make music
Music and rhyme
Rhyme, and you'll shine

~Just To You~

(The Minuet)

Thank you Lord for all your blessings
Blessings You send
Send to many
Many of us

Give us strength and courage today
Today, tomorrow
Tomorrow who knows
Knows what's to come

Help us in everything we do
Do everyday
Everyday pray
Pray just to you.

~Don't Know why~

(Hotan/Dodoitsu)

Don't know why people
Do bad things, and are so cruel
Think long and try understand
The reasons
Why some love to hurt
Even the ones that they love
And for no reason at all.

Trying to understand still
But I guess I never will
So many things we just can't
Man's sinful, life harden hearts.

~The Swan King~

(Key To My Heart)

Dream
Within
A dream
Breathless
Symphony
Castle********Of dreams
Romantic king of Bavaria
King Ludwig II was that
Yes was that and more
Tender hearted tortured soul
Unforgettable
His vision unique
Forever
A gift
that keeps
Giving
Thru the years
Misunderstood
Not mad
Sleep in
Peace sweet
King

My Sweet Love~
(Double Etheree)

My
Sweet love
There's something
That you just need
To know for long time
You're so important
To me, you make my heart glow
Every time I gaze in your eyes
It's like stepping back in time again
Your love makes me feel always so happy.

I want our love from now on just to grow
More and more, and never let you go
And forever this I just know
My sweet love there's something I
Want you to hear each and
Every day because
I love you my
Love now and
Always
Will.

~Mother's Greatest Love~

(Six Line poem)

Mother's
Job is
Never
Complete.
Mothers for their children always care.
With love for them everything they'd dare.

*
*
*
*
*

~Praying For You~

(Senryu Suit)

I'm praying for you
You have so much pain sorrows
but there's always hope

In Christ there's tomorrows
Just trust him and test his ways
he never leaves you

His mercy just shows
in him all it is possible
if you seek his light

Now heart bleeds for you
hoping that you find your way
each day for you pray

~Control~

(Free Style)

Learn to control yourself and you'll be fine
Losing control is bad, denotes lack of discipline
You can't control others but you can control the self
Why control others when you can't even control yourself

You can control many things like a regular machine
Controlling people, well that's another story
There are things and events that are out of our hands
Man can't control nature, so why try to get that glory

Giving advice is good to give to others if asked
But trying to control everything is simply a mistake
Trying to control other lives is just a foolish dream
Lack of control and discipline brings only heartache

Behavior and temper you should control all the time
When you're out of control you're not thinking fine
Lack of judgment comes from a mind out of control
Practice self-control and then your life will shine.

~Thank You Lord For A New Day~

(Nonet)

Release your magic and let it go
Flowers bloom and in the sun glow
Stand softly saluting day
Look with joy at the sky
Thank God when days done
Life is but one
Love with heart
And have
Fun.

*
*
*
*
*

~Believe~

(Carpe Diem)

Always just believe in yourself
And doing good my friend
Be positive
Just smile
Keep nice attitude with all around you

Just smile
And be happy
Bring his comfort and peace
Show good will and share his love
Be the best person you can be all time

*
*
*

~Nonet~

(Nonet)

The Nonet is a nice style to try
Let me tell you now that this form
It is kind of easy to do
I've done it many times
It's not hard at all
And it is fun
When you write
One.

*
*
*
*
*

~Heart~

(Senryu chain)

In him always find
Serenity, love and peace.
He lives in my heart.

When I call for him.
He is there for me in all.
He just makes me strong.

Foe might try hurt me.
But don't have to be afraid.
I know He's with me.

He's my solid rock.
In the dark He is my guide.
If I'm blind He's there.

~Beauty~

(Rictameter)

Beauty
Is all round us
Just creating beautiful
Memories with me and you too
See the sky so blue as the clouds drift by
Take a closer look today and
Find something nice in all
Just enjoy the
Beauty.

*
*
*
*
*

~Press Forward~

(Free style)

Keep climbing the mountain
Till you make it right to the top.
Believe that you can make it thru
And just never give up or stop.

You can accomplish anything
You desire in your heart to do.
Just believe it with all your might
And then you will make it thru.

Don't look back but press forward.
Don't stop and give up along the way.
Don't be afraid to stumble and fall sometimes.
Just focus your eyes on Jesus and pray.

He's right there with you today and every day.
Because God loves you and cares for you He says.

~And Then~

(Cinquain Double)

When you

Pray to God you

Will just feel it inside

And a wonderful peace will come

And then

And then

His love will show

And in his presence you'll

Be, and you'll feel His wonderful

Embrace.

~Day By Day~

(Quatern)

Day by day with God make my way.
With courage I need to do this.
I'll never quit no matter what.
I will hold my head high all time.

Rise walk thru all in spite of wrongs.
Day by day with God make my way.
In heart want to follow his plan.
That can be done I know can be.

Proceed with care with song in heart.
Within it I listen his voice.
Day by day with God make my way.
With him beside accomplish this.

Sometimes I have lots in my plate.
Always set goals where belong to.
With God and faith conquer fear all.
Day by day with God make my way.

~Memorial Day, A Day To Remember~

(Triolet)

Our fallen heroes just honor.
They served us well and gave their all.
Let's never forget, dishonor.
Our fallen heroes just honor.
Today they deserve great honor.
With much courage they answered call.
Our fallen heroes just honor.
They served us well and gave their all.

~Life~
(Tritina)

Learning new things everyday is fun.
There's always something new to learn.
Life's not easy all time I know.

But it's not just hard neither I know.
There are some things that can be fun.
Some things can be so hard to learn.

Many lessons in life to learn.
Life can make us grow quick we know.
So much pain sometimes, that's not fun.

Life can be fun, learn from it, know.

~Arguing~

(Anaphora)

Arguing can be just a terrible waste of time
Arguing brings bitter words from us in no time
Arguing can make sometimes things only worse
Arguing makes all of us angry and then start to curse
Arguing can get for us more than a point or two across
Arguing can make us very vulnerable and just cross
Arguing can do more than one positive or negative thing
Arguing no matter what, not a happy song in the end will sing
Arguing at the end may show that you're the one not that cool
Arguing is not right, better avoid a fight and don't argue with a fool
Arguing can hurt people you love bad, so better stop and walk away
Arguing when folks are not listening, is just a waste of time for me and you.

~My Love~

(Double Sedoka)

Hours tickle by and
Since you went away my Love
I can't stop thinking of you.
I love you so much
What more can I say to you?
You hold the key to my heart.

Life is not the same
Without you days are sadder.
I see more gray clouds in the
Sky each day I look.
My heart lost some of its shine,
Glad when I see you again.

~Growing Old~

(Quatern)

As we grow old we all slow down.
Our bodies go through many changes.
Metabolism slows down that too.
We lose muscle, some hair and teeth.

Nothing works the same when you're old.
As we grow old we all slow down.
As the body ages you get more tired.
Harder to get up, get going.

When getting old you lose your youth.
Most folks gain lots of wisdom too.
As we grow old we all slow down.
You forget more than used before.

Our children may all be grown up.
For senior's harder to move 'round.
We get wrinkles, gray hair, body hurts.
As we grow old we all slow down.

~Easy Or Hard~

(Quatern)

We can't have everything we want.
Some walk around with almost all.
While most folks don't even get some.
That's life and better accept it.

Can't force feeling on anyone.
We can't have everything we want.
You 're going to be loved or not.
The point is get with the program.

Life easy or hard you name it.
We make decisions along way.
We can't have everything we want.
Many folks win while the rest lose.

And that's the way all goes in life.
With God will make it thru rough times.
Loved or hated always be yourself.
We can't have everything we want.

~Sunshine~

(Rictameter)

Sunshine
There's a lot
During all the summer
But we might get lots of rain too
Sometimes it rains for days and days much more
Time to stay cool and have some fun
Folks are very happy
When they see the
Sunshine.

*
*
*
*
*

~Living Life~

(Quatern)

Experiences earned from living life.
You can read but are you learning?
Everything in life has price tag.
You can't pass tests without fire.

Don't look out too much see inside.
Experiences earned from living life.
When life throw you rocks make a soup.
Turn page of book when done go next.

Nothing in this life last forever.
Look 'round twice do you see things same?
Experiences earned from living life.
Make peace with self don't look back.

Life's school of learning every day.
Are you learning from your mistakes?
When life hand you lemons make juice.
Experiences earned from living life.

~Master Painters~
(Cinquain Suit)

Paintings
Some beautiful
Masterpieces to enjoy
The Mona Lisa with that smile of hers
Arcane

Arcane
Delightful ones
Paintings that bring much joy
Rembrandt, Vermeer, Van Goth, Kinkade
Masters

Masters
Of great paintings
God given gifts that glows
Study their work looking at them
Bring joy

Bring joy
Many stand time
Bob Ross great painter too
Leonardo Dali just mention few are
All great.

*

*

~Forgive~

(Pantoum)

When folks are mean, just let it go
In silence forgive, then move on
Sometimes is best to go with flow
Anger brings pain none good to show.

In silence forgive, then move on
Not easy, but right thing to do
Anger brings pain none good to show
Allow no one make your day just blue.

Not easy, but right thing to do
Sometimes is best to go with flow
Allow no one turn your day just blue
When folks are mean, just let it go.

~Lost~

(Tanka)

We all make mistakes
And that's the way that it goes
Many things go wrong
Some folks are not bad just lost
Often we all lose our way.

*
*
*
*
*

~Imagination~

(Triolet)

Books are just really awesome
They just open so many doors
With books you can learn lots at home
Books are just really awesome
Read diverse subjects and poems
They have so much for you in store
Books are just really awesome
They just open so many doors.

~Far From Home~

(Blessed Cross)

God can protect us from any harm
Having Him better than any charm
His Word says we're never alone
No matter close or far from home.

Nobody knows when our time on earth will just end
Won't you come to Him today as you are my friend
Just accept His salvation as to Him you pray
Jesus can't and won't force you in any which way.

Once you repent invite Him in
Receive His gift He'll wash your sin
He offers salvation to all
Make sure you heed His loving call.

No one else can do this but you
God will help you in all you do
Far from home but not from Father
If you don't have Him life's harder.

God can protect us from any harm
Once you repent invite Him in
No one else can do this but you
Having Him is better than any charm
Receive His gift He'll wash your sin
God will help you in all you do.

~Remember~

(Rhyming Couplets)

Just reach every single night and day
For God and all the stars in the sky.

There's always a brand new day to look to
When you can close some of your wounds too.

Just look forward to watching next day shows
Meanwhile be happy of having today before it goes.

It is very nice to see every day the sunrise
And the sunset in the pretty sky just rise.

Sometimes we don't appreciate enough what we have to
So enjoy, remember that nothing last forever and that's true.

~OH LORD HELP ME~

(WHITNEY)

OH LORD HIDE
ME FROM MY FOES
HELP ME GROW
IN ALL JUST GLOW
LET IT SHOW
OH LORD MY GOD
YOU'RE MY ROCK AND WALKING ROD.

*

*

*

~CONCERNING DOGS AND CATS~

(RHYMING COUPLETS)

I DO REALLY LIKE DOGS AND CATS
AND I LOVE TO WEAR A GOOD HAT.

I KNOW I COULD TRIP OVER A MAT
IF ALL OF SUDDEN I SAW A BIG AND NASTY RAT.

SOMETIMES THINGS CAN BE SUCH A DRAT
MY HEAD HURTS AS I HOLDING IT HERE SAT.

NEED TO RELAX NOW BUT HERE AGAIN COMES MY CAT
SHE WANTS TO EAT MORE AND MORE AND THATS WHY SHE'S SO FAT.

I ALWAYS WONDER WHY DOGS AND CATS FIGHT
ONE SCRATCHES AND THE OTHER ONE CAN BITE.

DOGS AND CATS CAN MAKE YOUR LIFE MORE BRIGHT
THEY'RE A LOT BETTER AND EASIER THAN FLYING A KITE.

THEY GIVE TO US SO MANY WONDERFUL JOYS AND REWARDS
AND FOR US THEY HAVE A TREASURE TROVE ALWAYS STORED.

DOGS AND CATS CAN BE VERY GOOD PETS AND FRIENDS TO ALL MEN
TREAT THEM WITH ALL YOUR LOVE AND RESPECT AND YOU SHALL SEE GREAT RESULTS THEN.

SOME PEOPLE PREFER DOGS AND FOR SOME ARE THE CATS THAT MAKE BEST FRIENDS
BUT SOME FOLKS ARE SO MEAN NOT EVEN WITH A PET A GOOD TIME THEY CAN SPEND.

LIKE I SAY AND BELIEVE ALL THESE MANY YEARS IT'S ALL UP TO YOU IN THE END
SO WHATEVER YOU CHOOSE DON'T WHINE BECAUSE NO ONE WANTS TO BE THEN YOUR FRIEND.

~A HAPPY MOTHER'S DAY POEM~

(TRINE)

THERE'S NO OTHER LOVE LIKE A MOTHER
SHE LOVES YOU SO MUCH LIKE NO OTHER.

MOTHERS ARE ANGELS FROM GOD SENT TO EARTH.
THEY'RE HERE FOR US SINCE MOMENT OF BIRTH.

MOTHERS JUST WANT WITH US SO MUCH TO SHARE.
THEY GIVE US THEIR LOVE AND FOR US THEY CARE.

YOUR MOTHER LOVES YOU MORE THAN ANY SISTER OR BROTHER.
MOTHERS ARE SO IMPORTANT, MORE THAN ANY GOLD THEY'RE WORTH.
MOTHERS ARE A BLESSING FROM GOD WHO FOR US REALLY CARES.

~GOOD ANGELS~

(TRIOLET)

ANGELS FOR SURE ARE JUST DIVINE.
APPEAR IN MANY FORMS AND SHAPES.
SENT FROM GOD TO US, WHICH IS FINE.
ANGELS FOR SURE ARE JUST DIVINE.
WHEN THEY COME MAKE OUR DAY JUST SHINE.
THEY HELP OUT OF DANGER ESCAPE.
ANGELS FOR SURE ARE JUST DIVINE.
APPEAR IN MANY FORMS AND SHAPES.

~MY HOPE~
(NONET)

I MEDITATE AND HOPE YOU SOON COME
THERE'S CHAOS,MANY FOLKS IN PAIN NUMB
IF YOU DON'T, WHAT OF US BECOME
THERE'S SADNESS AND MUCH GLUM
I BELIEVE YOU'RE NEAR
WITH YOU NO FEAR
YOU DRY TEARS
AND BRING
CHEERS.

*

*

~SO BEAUTIFULLY~

(THE TREE)

NICE
WONDROUS
CHRISTMAS TREE
SO FULL OF LIGHT
GOD'S LOVE GIVING DELIGHT
HAPPY FACES JUST GLOWING
DURING CHRISTMAS LOVE SHOWING
SO BEAUTIFULLY SHINES AT NIGHT
N
I
C
E
WONDROUS.

~ROSES ARE~

(FIVE SENSES POETRY)

ROSES ARE RED,YELLOW,PINK.
ROSES TASTE LIKE STRAWBERRIES 'N CREAM.
ROSES SOUND LIKE CLAUDE DEBUSSY CLAIRE DE LUNE.
ROSES SMELL LIKE A (COCO) CHANEL NO. 5 PERFUME.
ROSES LOOK LIKE A THOMAS KINKADE PAINTING.
ROSES MAKE ME HAPPY AND FEEL WARM AND LOVED.

~I RATHER~

(ANAPHORA)

I RATHER BE HAPPY ANYTIME THAN SAD
I RATHER BE GLAD THAN OFTEN MAD
I RATHER BE WRITING THAN CLEANING
I RATHER BE READING THAN SLEEPING
I RATHER SEE FLOWERS AND ROSES BLOOM
I RATHER GET RID OF ALL THIS DAY'S GLOOM
I RATHER WATCH SUNRISES SHOW UP IN THE SKY
I RATHER SPEND A LOT OF TIME WITH YOU
I RATHER TALK OVER THE PHONE THAN SEND A LETTER
I'D RATHER BE VERY CALM THAN PLAIN SCARED.

~THE WHOLE DAY~

(OCTAZ-RHYME)

THE WHOLE DAY
CAN BE SO MUCH FUN
LETS GO OUTSIDE ENJOY THE SUN
THIS A FINE SPRING DAY FOR YOU TO ENJOY
DON'T LET THINGS RUIN YOUR JOY
STEP OUT THE WRONG PLATE
AND WALK LINE STRAIGHT.

~COUNT ALL YOUR BLESSINGS EVERYDAY~

(KYRIELLE)

MAKE ALL YOUR DREAMS FOR YOU JUST SHINE
DON'T LOOK BACK JUST WALK STRAIGHT THE LINE
CELEBRATE YOUR LIFE ALL THE WAY
COUNT ALL YOUR BLESSINGS EVERYDAY.

MAKE ALL YOUR DREAMS COME TRUE AND GLOW
ENJOY LIFE TO FULLEST AND GROW
REMEMBER THAT GOD LOVES YOU TOO
COUNT ALL YOUR BLESSINGS EVERYDAY.

KEEP ALL YOUR THOUGHTS POSITIVE AND PURE
MAKE IMPORTANT DECISIONS TILL YOU'RE SURE
TAKE GOOD LOOK AND BE TRUE TO YOU
COUNT ALL YOUR BLESSINGS EVERYDAY.
DON'T STRAY.

~REMINDERS~

(RHYMING COUPLETS)

GOD IS REALLY THE ONE IN CONTROL OF THIS PLANET AND NOT ANY MAN AT ALL.
STILL HE GIVES US FREEDOM TO MAKE RIGHT OR WRONG DECISIONS,HE'S THERE WHEN WE FALL.

HE HAS FOR SURE YOUR LIFE AND MINE IN HIS HANDS AND CAN DO FOR US ANYTHING.
BUT STILL WE HAVE RESPONSIBILITIES TO DO CHOICES,AND DO OUR OWN DREAMS AND THING.

WITH GOD BY MY SIDE I DON'T HAVE TO WORRY TOO MUCH,WITH HIM I DON'T HAVE TO CRAWL.
WITH HIM I FEEL SO SECURE,I KNOW HE PROTECTS ME ALL THE WAY AND SAFE WILL BE MY SOUL.

GOD'S KINGDOM HAS NO BEGINNING AND NEITHER WILL EVER HAVE HERE OR ANYWHERE AN END.
THERE IS AN IMPORTANT THING TO REMEMBER,IN HIM YOU AND I CAN ALWAYS HAVE A BEST FRIEND.

HE HAS CREATED EVERYTHING THAT IS GOOD AND IN HIS IMAGE MADE YOU AND ME,AND ALL MEN.
IN MY LIFE I ALWAYS TRY TO PUT GOD FIRST AND THANK AND PRAISE HIM ON MY KNEES EVERYDAY.AMEN.

I JUST THANK HIM AND PRAISE HIM EVERYDAY FOR ALL, EVERY SINGLE DAY AND EVERY NIGHT.
WITHOUT HIM AND HIS LOVE THERE WOULDN'T BE FOR ME OR ANY OF US ANY LOVE AND LIGHT.

HE OFFERS AND ALWAYS GIVES US ALL HIS LOVE,HIS FORGIVENESS,SALVATION AND PEACE.
FOR ME HIS WORDS SHALL NEVER PASS,AND ALSO HIS LOVE AND MERCY SHALL NEVER CEASE.

GOD, HE'S ALWAYS MY BRIGHTEST STAR AND WILL SURELY GUIDE ME STRAIGHT AND THROUGH I PRAY.
AND WITH HIM BY MY SIDE ON THE RIGHT PATH I SHALL WALK ON AND HE'LL LIGHT MY WAY.

~SOMETIMES THE DAYS~
(BALLOON)

SOME
TIMES THE
DAYS ARE SHORT
SOMETIMES THE DAYS
ARE LONG,SOMETIMES NOTHING'S RIGHT
EVERYTHING TENDS TO GO WRONG
AND TIMES I WONDER WHY
THIS AND THAT HAPPENS
SOMETIMES DO NOTHING
JUST ABOUT IT
BUT TURN BLIND EYE
TO ALL
THE
THINGS
WE
FEEL
SEE
SOME DON'T WORK ENOUGH
TO MAKE THINGS BETTER
SOMETIMES FOLKS WANT WAR
REJECT PEACE. SOME DAYS
CAN BE GOOD OR BAD.

~SPRING RAINS~

(AMERICAN DIAMANTES SUIT)

IT
IS RAINING
THE WHOLE DAY
THE DAY IS GLOOMY
RAIN DOESN'T STOP
FOR MANY
HOURS.

DARK
CLOUDS ADORN
THE GRAY SKY
PLAYING HAVOC WITH US.
DEWDROPS FALL FROM
LEAVES AND
PETALS.

OUTSIDE
IS WET
IT'S COLD.RAIN
REFRESHES ALL AROUND,BUT
NO FUN WHEN
RAINS TOO
MUCH.

~WHEN IT SEEMS~

(THE TREE)

WHEN
YOU'RE LOST
AND SEE DREAMS
GO WRONG JUST ASK
THE MASTER FOR HELP
HE'LL HELP YOU BE STRONG WHEN
TROUBLES PILE HIGH ASK MASTER
HE'LL GIVE YOU AGAIN DREAMS AND HOPES.
W
H
E
N
YOU'RE LOST.

~SO MANY THINGS~

(FREE STYLE)

THERE ARE SO MANY THINGS TO WRITE ABOUT
AND SO MANY BEAUTIFUL THINGS TO SEE WHEN I GO OUT
I SEE TOO MANY FLOWERS DURING SPRING BLOOM
THE SKY IS SO BLUE,NOWHERE THERE'S BLOOM.

I SIT DOWN AT LAST AND I THINK JUST OF YOU
AND OF ALL THE THINGS YOU WISH ME TO DO
THERE'S NO TIME TO WASTE, BE STRESSED OR SAD
I RATHER BE SMILING AND BECAUSE OF YOU GLAD.

LIFE CAN BE SO HARD SO MANY TIMES
AND SOMETIMES NOTHING I DO GOES FINE
THERE ARE SO MANY THINGS TO WRITE ABOUT
AND SO MANY BEAUTIFUL THINGS TO SEE WHEN I GO OUT.

~YOU LIFT ME UP~

(TRINE)

WHEN TROUBLES BLOW MY WAY AND JUST COME
YOU HELP ME SEE BETTER AND THEN SOME.

YOU LIFT MY SPIRIT UP AND MY SOUL LIKE NO ONE CAN
YOU'RE MY SAVIOR AND YOU WANT TO SAVE EVERY MAN.

WITH YOU I DON'T HAVE TO WALK ANYMORE ALONE
AND I KNOW THAT YOU LOVE ME JUST LIKE NO ONE.

YOU GIVE ME SERENITY AND PEACE WHEN MY THOUGHTS
JUST ROAM.
YOU HEAL MY BROKEN HEART AND YOU HAVE FOR ME THE
PERFECT PLAN
I'M SO HAPPY ONE DAY I'LL STAND AND PRAISE IN FRONT OF
YOUR THRONE.

~TODAY IS A GIFT FROM GOD~

(DIAMANTES)

TODAY
IS A
GIFT WHICH CAN
DISSAPEAR IN A MOMENT'S
TIME,LIFE CAN
BE JUST
SHORT.

SO
ENJOY ALL
TIME YOU HAVE
LIFE TOO SHORT TO
LIVE JUST SAD
SMILE, BE
HAPPY!

NO
ONE KNOWS
HOW LONG WE
HAVE SO BETTER ENJOY
MAKE BEST OF
EVERYTHING AND
ALL.

About the Author

Dorian Petersen Potter has been writing poetry for most of her life. Her poetry has been published in many anthologies and poetry collections all over the world. Her poetry today can be found in many places in the internet and in several of her poetry pages too.

Dorian's personal websites:

"Poetic Dreams"

http://www.PoetryPoem.com/ladydp2000

and

http://publishing with passion.com/dorianpetersenpotter.html

www.ingramcontent.com/pod-product-compliance
Ingram Content Group UK Ltd.
Pitfield, Milton Keynes, MK11 3LW, UK
UKHW041837200726
13854UKWH00003BA/1192

9 781300 320739